My Family

MY FAMILY

Ordinary Memories of
Extraordinary People

Compiled by
Rob Parsons and Fiona Castle

Hodder & Stoughton
LONDON SYDNEY AUCKLAND

The right of Rob Parsons and Fiona Castle to be identified as the
editors of this work has been asserted in accordance with the
Copyright, Designs and Patents Act 1988.

Apart from a massive thank you to all the celebrities,
special thanks to Tom Beardshaw, Jonathan Booth
and Peter Dymond.

1 3 5 7 9 10 8 6 4 2

British Library Cataloguing in Publication Data:
A record for this book is available from the British Library.

ISBN 0 340 72197 9

Typeset in CA Manticore by
Strathmore Publishing Services, London N7

Printed and bound in Great Britain by
Biddles Ltd, Guildford and King's Lynn

Hodder and Stoughton Ltd,
A division of Hodder Headline PLC,
338 Euston Road, London NW1 3BH

Dedications

To my mum and sisters, Val and Joan
— ROB PARSONS

In gratitude to God for the wonderful family
He has given me
— FIONA CASTLE

*T*HIS *volume began life as a celebration of the tenth anniversary of* CARE FOR THE FAMILY, *a national charity that Roy Castle cared deeply about. But as the contributions came in from celebrities from all over the world we realised it was far wider than that.* MY FAMILY *is a celebration of family life generally – its joy, heartache, laughter and hair-pulling-out frustration!*

Families can be funny things; they sometimes contain those we love the most and find the hardest to get on with. And yet there is often a very hardy emotion within families – a "there when the chips are down" kind of love and perhaps above all the wonder that those who know us best still care for us. And this fact changes little whether you are an "ordinary" mum or dad, or a world-famous athlete, writer, politician or movie star. It may be that such bonds are even more precious when you are living in the public gaze; family members can be the few people who can look beyond the public image to see the person that you really are. The strength of families is that they have decided to love you before reading your reviews (and still love you even after reading them!).

This book is an attempt to tell a very ordinary story through the lives of some extraordinary people: people who have become household names, and yet to their mums and

7

dads, their wives, husbands and children, they are as close and as "ordinary" as we are to our families.

There is a wonderful variety here, from Kenny Dalglish's simple memory of the birth of his children to Nelson Mandela's recollection of learning at his mother's knee. And, as with all families, there are memories that will bring a smile to your face, and others that will enable you to feel a little of the pain that someone you know only through the media has faced.

Perhaps there never was a "golden age" of family life. We are certainly not experiencing one today; and yet the family is still the place where we learn our basic skills and form beliefs that often remain with us for a lifetime. Sometimes we fool ourselves that we have broken free from our roots; only to discover that the old influences are stronger than we thought. Families matter.

There will be many different kinds of people who read this book. Some will have very happy memories of childhood, while others will recall events that still bring hurt. Some will have known the trauma of family break-up. You will find many of these experiences reflected in the pages of this book, for not all the memories presented here are happy ones. But whatever your circumstances, we hope that this anthology of memories will remind you of how special families are and of the commitment of charities like CARE FOR THE FAMILY *which exist to help them in crisis and strengthen them in the good times.*

So put the coffee on and prepare to peek into the lives of the famous and to observe the rich diversity of family life - the amazing, humdrum, cataclysmic and everyday events that make families what they are. But above all prepare to have your own memories rekindled.

ROB PARSONS *and* FIONA CASTLE

P.S.   We know we're not "extraordinary", but we are the editors, so we took the liberty of putting a couple of our own memories in!

Contents

Gloria Hunniford 14

Nelson Mandela 16

Edwina Currie 18

Richard Branson 20

Ian Botham 25

Bill Cosby 27

Michael Fish 30

Paddy Ashdown 32

David Frost 34

Michael Parkinson 36

John Major 40

Jeffrey Archer 42

Ann Widdecombe 46

Tony Blair 48

Colin Dexter 50

Carol Vorderman 52

David Puttnam 54

Patrick Moore 56

David Alton 58

Michael Palin 61

Kenny Dalglish 65

Dickie Bird 67

Fiona Castle 69

Sally Gunnell 72

My Family

Frank Bruno 74

Ian McCaskill 76

Lynda Lee-Potter 78

William Hague 82

Jilly Cooper 84

Pam Rhodes 86

Richard Madeley and Judy Finnigan 89

Jane Asher 92

Harry Secombe 94

Alex Ferguson 96

Diane Louise Jordan 99

Martine McCutcheon 102

John Harvey-Jones 104

Spike Milligan 106

Roy Castle 108

Kevin Keegan 112

John Cole 115

Rob Parsons 117

Jonathan Edwards 120

Sources 123

A note about Care for the Family 125

MY FAMILY

Ordinary Memories of
Extraordinary People

Gloria Hunniford

GLORIA HUNNIFORD was born into an Irish family in 1940. She is a radio and television presenter, who is especially well-known for the panel quiz show *We Love TV* and for her work on Radio 2.

Think of your greatest hero; the one person that you would most like to meet. It could be a musician, a great thinker or an artist. Once, they too were small children, running around the feet of their mum or dad. Now imagine the parents of your hero, seeing the burgeoning talent of their child begin to enthral those around them, and their glow of pride in realising just how special their child is going to be. It is a feeling that every parent shares with each small success of their children ...

Gloria Hunniford

I was sitting with Cliff Richard's mother at
Wembley Stadium one evening as we watched
him perform in concert when she suddenly smiled
and said, "You know, I'm so proud of him". It struck
me how strange it must have felt for her, as though
she was on the outside looking in. Here was this
man she'd given birth to, changed his nappies, now
all grown up and filling Wembley on eighteen con-
secutive nights. Most of the world never thinks of a
celebrity as someone's child – it's the secret every
mother carries with her, but if she's lucky, now and
then she'll get a chance to crow about it.

Nelson Mandela

NELSON MANDELA is the son of a chief of the Tembu tribe who was born in 1918. He trained and practised as a lawyer before becoming one of the leaders of the African National Congress (ANC) and a key figure in the struggle against apartheid. Convicted of treason, he was imprisoned on Robben Island from 1964 to 1990. Four years after his release he became President of the new South Africa. He has received numerous honorary degrees and international awards, including the Nobel Peace Prize in 1993. He married for the third time on his eightieth birthday in 1998 and has two daughters by an earlier marriage.

Families are often the places where we learn the truly important lessons of life; where we begin to understand what the world is like, our place in it and a sense of how to live. As we read the following story of a mother faithfully passing on stories to educate her young son, we wondered whether she could have had any idea that the child at her knee would change the world.

*A*FTER games ... I would return to my mother's kraal where she was preparing supper. Whereas my father once told stories of historic battles and heroic Xhosa warriors, my mother would enchant us with Xhosa legends and fables that had come down from numberless generations. These tales stimulated my childish imagination, and usually contained some moral lesson.

I recall one my mother told us about a traveller who was approached by an old woman with terrible cataracts on her eyes. The woman asked the traveller for help, and he averted his eyes. Then another man came along and was approached by the old woman. She asked him to clean her eyes, and even though he found the task unpleasant, he did as she asked. Then, miraculously, the scales fell from the woman's eyes and she became young and beautiful. The man married her and became wealthy and prosperous. It is a simple tale, but its message is an enduring one: virtue and generosity will be rewarded in ways that one cannot know.

Edwina Currie

EDWINA CURRIE is married to Raymond and has two daughters. From 1983 to 1997 she was MP for Derbyshire South. She now writes novels, contributes regularly to the media, and pursues her strong interest in European affairs.

*I*T took my daughter Debbie a long time to arrive. All night, in fact; and we forgot, later, how much pain and striving it takes to bring a child into the world.

Somewhere around 5.00 a.m. the consultant sighed deeply. "Into the theatre with you", he muttered. "This child's getting stuck. Big-headed family, are you?"

My husband went slightly green. In fact the next time I saw him he was green all over, gowned from head to foot.

But by then the baby was in my arms, born by ventouse extraction, a big, purple bruise on her forehead and her eyes shut tight against the light; for outside, dawn was breaking, and turning her little nose pink and gold. So I called her "Debbie Dewdrop" because she came with the dawn; and twenty-three years on, she is still lovely.

Richard Branson

RICHARD BRANSON is the son of a leading lawyer and a magistrate. Born on 18 July 1950, he showed entrepreneurial flair while still at school, and now has wide-ranging business interests in his Virgin Group, which includes trains, a radio station, an airline, music, travel, hotels, communications and retail. He married Joan in 1989 and they have a son and a daughter. In 1991 he held the world record for the longest flight and the fastest speed in a hot-air balloon.

M y childhood is something of a blur to me now, but there are several episodes that stand out. I do remember that my parents continually set us challenges. My mother was determined to make us independent. When I was four years old, she stopped the car a few miles from our house and made me find my own way home across the fields. I got helplessly lost.

My youngest sister Vanessa's earliest memory is being woken up in the dark one January morning. Mum packed some sandwiches and an apple and told me to find some water along the way. Bournemouth was fifty miles away from our home in Shamley Green, Surrey. I was under twelve, but

Mum thought that it would teach me the import-
ance of stamina and a sense of direction. I remember setting off in the dark, and I have a vague
recollection of staying the night with a relative. I
have no idea how I found their house, or how I got
back to Shamley Green the next day, but I do
remember finally walking into the kitchen like a
conquering hero, feeling tremendously proud of my
marathon bike ride and expecting a huge welcome.

"Well done, Ricky", Mum greeted me in the
kitchen, where she was chopping onions. "Was that
fun? Now could you run along to the vicar's? He's
got some logs he wants chopping and I told him
that you'd be back any minute."

Our challenges tended to be physical rather than
academic, and soon we were setting them for ourselves. I have an early memory of learning to swim.
I was either four or five, and we had been on holiday in Devon with Dad's sisters, Auntie Joyce and
Aunt Wendy, and Wendy's husband, Uncle Joe. I
was particularly fond of Auntie Joyce, and at the
beginning of the holiday she had bet me ten
shillings that I couldn't learn to swim by the end of
the fortnight. I spent hours in the sea trying to
swim against the freezing-cold waves, but by the
last day I still couldn't do it. I just splashed along

with one foot hopping on the bottom. I'd lunge forward and crash beneath the waves before spluttering up to the surface trying not to swallow the sea-water.

"Never mind, Ricky", Auntie Joyce said. "There's always next year."

But I was determined not to wait that long. Auntie Joyce had made me a bet, and I doubted that she would remember it the next year. On our last day we got up early, packed the cars and set out on the twelve-hour journey home. The roads were narrow; the cars were slow; and it was a hot day. Everyone wanted to get home. As we drove along I saw a river.

"Daddy, can you stop the car, please?" I said.

The river was my last chance; I was sure that I could swim and win Auntie Joyce's ten shillings.

"Please stop!" I shouted.

Dad looked in the rear-view mirror, slowed down and pulled up on the grass verge.

"What's the matter?" Aunt Wendy complained. "It's such a long drive."

"Come on, Wendy. Let's give the lad a chance", Auntie Joyce said. "After all, it's *my* ten shillings."

I pulled off my clothes and ran down to the riverbank in my underpants. I didn't dare stop in case anyone changed their minds. By the time that I reached the water's edge I was rather frightened. Out in the middle of the river, the water was flowing fast with a stream of bubbles dancing over the boulders. I found a part of the bank that had been trodden down by some cows, and waded out into the current. The mud squeezed up between my toes. I looked back. Uncle Joe and Aunt Wendy, Auntie Joyce, my parents and sister Lindi stood watching me, the ladies in floral dresses, the men in sports jackets and ties. Dad was lighting his pipe and looking utterly unconcerned; Mum was smiling her usual encouragement.

I braced myself and jumped forward against the current, but I immediately felt myself sinking, my legs slicing uselessly through the water. The current pushed me around, tore at my underpants and dragged me downstream. I couldn't breathe and I swallowed water. I tried to reach up to the surface, but had nothing to push against. I kicked and writhed around but it was no help.

Then my foot found a stone and I pushed up hard. I came back above the surface and took a deep breath. The breath steadied me, and I relaxed. I had to win that ten shillings.

I kicked slowly, spread my arms, and found

myself swimming across the surface. I took a deep breath. I was still bobbing up and down, but I suddenly felt released: I could swim. I didn't care that the river was pulling me downstream. I swam triumphantly out into the middle of the current. Above the roar and bubble of the water I heard my family clapping and cheering. As I swam in a lop-sided circle and came back to the riverbank some fifty yards below them, I saw Auntie Joyce fish in her huge black handbag for her purse. I crawled up out of the water, brushed through a patch of stinging nettles and ran up the bank. I may have been cold, muddy and stung by the nettles, but I could swim.

"Here you are, Ricky," Auntie Joyce said. "Well done."

I looked at the ten shilling note in my hand. It was large, brown and crisp. I had never held that amount of money before; it seemed a fortune.

"All right, everyone", Dad said. "On we go."

It was then that I realised that he too was dripping wet. He had lost his nerve and dived in after me. He gave me a massive hug.

Ian Botham

IAN BOTHAM OBE is married to Kathryn and they have a son and two daughters. The most charismatic and inspiring cricketer of his generation, Ian played for England from 1977 to 1992, captained the team in 1980–81 and scored 5,200 runs and took 383 wickets and 120 catches in 102 Tests. He is now a TV cricket commentator, appears regularly in pantomime and is well known for his marathon walks in aid of leukaemia research.

Separation from our families is hard and perhaps especially so when we miss the birth of a child. A cricketing legend shares how he coped.

*B*EING one of four children and having three of my own, plus nieces and nephews, family memories are many.

Over the years my sporting life took me away from home for long periods of time and when the children were young I had to be content with photos and stories from home. Out of our three children, Liam, Sarah and Becky, I was only at home for the birth of our son way back in 1977. Sarah was born in

1979 while I was touring with England "down under" and Becky in 1985 while I was walking the length of Britain for charity.

In February 1998, I was in the West Indies commentating on England's cricketing exploits when my grandson James Ian was born. I had had the champagne on ice for weeks in various parts of the West Indies; and two weeks and several hundreds of pounds worth of phone bills later he made his appearance, all 11 lb of him. What a feeling! Grandad Beefy. Well we'll just drop the grandad part, please.

Time goes on, my lifestyle changes little but the memories grow, and I look forward to years of pleasure with my grandsons, Regan and James, and grandchildren still to come.

Bill Cosby

BILL COSBY was born on 12 July 1938. He was the first black actor in America to get equal star billing in a TV series, and has gone on to become one of the USA's greatest entertainers. Best known in Britain for *The Cosby Show*, Bill is married to Camille and they have four children. Their son Ennis was tragically murdered.

Some people say that childhood is the best time of your life, others say that you never realise this until it is too late! Whatever our experience, as Bill Cosby tells us, childhood has a profound impact on the rest of our lives.

THE French like to say, "The more things change, the more they stay the same". These words do not, of course, refer to the birth of a butterfly, but they do refer to childhood, which has basically been the same ever since Cain decided he wanted to be an only child. The only difference between the childhood I experienced and childhood today is that I didn't expect my parents to be social directors for me. I never once said I was bored, for children began to be bored only in June of 1963. I was a boy at a time when kids endlessly amused themselves, when a toddler exercise class was one toddler pounding another.

Today's child tells his parents, "You brought me here. Now entertain me."

If I had ever said these words to my father, he would have smilingly replied, "Yes, I brought you here and I can take you out and I can make another that's got to be better."

However, he didn't take me out: he let me finish childhood and then go on to get married and turn my own five children loose on an unprepared world.

It is popular today to say that we have to find the child within us. For me, this would be a short search.

I am 54 now, but I am still the kid who put the snowball in my mother's freezer so that, one summer day, I could hit my brother with what he thought was a new ice age. I am still the kid who believed that Dracula lived not in Transylvania but Pennsylvania. And I am still the kid who fell so dizzily in love with a sixth-grade girl when I was a school-crossing guard that I almost waved her under a bus.

No matter how old I am, these memories will always be with me, just as your own childhood is probably clearer in your mind than the place where you left your glasses.

Michael Fish

MICHAEL FISH was born in Eastbourne on 27 April 1944 and is Britain's longest-serving weather forecaster on television and radio. A Fellow of the Royal Meteorological Society, he is best known for assuring viewers that the 1987 hurricane was not about to happen – a fame he accepts with wry good humour. He is married to Susan and they have two daughters.

The birth of a sister inspired a young member of Michael Fish's family, as he explains in this Christmas memory:

A Special Family Memory

My younger daughter, Nicola, was born at the
end of November twenty-two years ago when
Alison, my elder daughter, was four-and-a-half
years old. As it was very close to Christmas,
rehearsals for the school nativity play were in
full swing and Alison practised her songs all the
time. It was her first Christmas at school and
she was nearly as excited about the nativity play
as she was about the arrival of her new baby
sister! I took her into the hospital to meet Nicola
for the first time and after a few moments she
stood by the crib and sang "Away in a manger".

Having been there to witness both my daughters
being born, this brought an additional lump to
my throat and is a memory both my wife and I
have always treasured.

Michael Fish   21.5.98

Paddy Ashdown

THE RT HON. PADDY ASHDOWN MP served with the Royal
Marines from 1959 to 1971, followed by five years as part of the
UK mission to the United Nations in Geneva. Since 1983 he
has been MP for Yeovil and became Leader of the Liberal
Democrats in 1988. Born on 27 February 1941, he married Jane
in 1962 and they have a son and a daughter. His hobbies
include wine-making.

M Y earliest memory of my own family dates from
the time I was about five years old. My father
was an Indian Army Officer and the family had been
in India for 200 years. When the British left India,
we went from our home in the north-west provinces
down to the coast. The date was, I believe, 1946 and
the early partition riots had started. The memory,
which often haunted me later as nightmares in my
youth, was of a very overcrowded and hot train, on
an Indian siding on our way down to the coast. I can
remember a sense of fear in the train and of horror,
and a strange and pervasive smell. The train waited
for what seemed an age, eventually pulling slowly
forward through an Indian station with two long
platforms covered with mutilated bodies. My mother

tried to hide my eyes, but I managed to peep out. Ever since that day I have been unable to ignore ethnic conflict, and on visiting places such as Bosnia and Kosovo, this memory remains with me. It reminds me of my fortune in being able to live at a time of peace without having to fear for my family.

On a lighter note, my happiest family memories are of the time I was serving as a diplomat in Geneva. We lived in a massive house on the shores of Lake Geneva, an almost entirely sybaritic life. I kept myself fit. I was able to come home in the evening to read to my kids; we went sailing on our yacht, which was at the end of the pier that ran out from our house; we went skiing in the winter; I took my kids walking and climbing in the mountains in the summer, and I was able to climb Mont Blanc. I look back on these times as the halcyon days of my life.

David Frost

SIR DAVID FROST was born on 7 April 1939, the son of a clergyman. A television presenter, interviewer, author, cricket fan and joint founder of London Weekend Television, he is particularly remembered by many for *That Was the Week That Was* and *The Frost Programme*. In 1983 he married Lady Carina Fitzalan-Howard and they have three sons. He was knighted in 1993.

Sometimes, exploring life can throw up some very unexpected surprises ...

MY earliest childhood memory is of Brinklows, a small general store in Kempston. At approximately the age of two, I was sitting in a pushchair outside the said Brinklows when I spotted a container of mustard in my mother's basket, which was hanging from the pushchair. I managed to get it open, and tried to swallow all the mustard down in one great swig.

The taste was horrendous, and to this day I have never been able to touch even a smidgen of mustard.

Fortunately, Sir David recovered, although out of one danger and into another – this time an identity crisis ...

*I*N the garden at Kempston, I would assemble imaginary cricket teams, and my luckless sisters, their boyfriends and my father would bowl to me. When I was out, I would retire to the woodshed and emerge as the next batsman. "Who are you now?" the bowlers would ask wearily. As often as possible, my reply would be "Bill Edrich" or "Dennis Compton".

Michael Parkinson

MICHAEL PARKINSON was born on 28 March 1935. Though his name is synonymous with the chat show, he is also a much-loved sports writer. He is married to Mary and they have three sons.

> He was a man, take him all in all, I shall not look upon
> his like again.   – *Hamlet of his father*

Michael remembers a miner who was "a remarkable man".

MY OLD MAN

I was never told fairy-tales as a child. Instead I heard of Larwood's action and Hobbs's perfection. Before I ever saw him play I knew Len Hutton intimately, and the first time I witnessed Stanley Matthews in the flesh I knew which way he was going even if the full-back didn't. The stories of these gods, and many, many more besides I heard at my father's knee.

He was a remarkable man with a marvellous facility to adorn an anecdote. It was he who invented the gate, complete with attendant, which was built in honour of a Barnsley winger who could run like the wind but didn't know how to stop. At the end of one of his runs down the wing the gate would be open and the winger would career through and out of the ground to finally come to a stop halfway across the car-park. Or so Dad said.

It was he who told me of the full-back whose fearsome sliding tackles carried him into the wall surrounding the ground causing the spectators to start wearing goggles at home games for fear of being blinded by flying chips of concrete. Frank Barson, he assured me, once ran the entire length of the field bouncing the ball on his head, beat the opposing goalkeeper, and then headed his final effort over the crossbar because he'd had a row with the manager before the game.

Moreover, the old man swore he managed to see Len Hutton's 364 at the Oval by convincing the gate attendant that he was dying of some incurable disease and his last wish was to see Len before he took leave of this earth. I never swallowed that one until once at a football match where the gates were closed I witnessed him convince a gateman that he was a journalist and I was his runner. I was seven at the time, and it was the very first occasion I watched a football match from a press box.

Of all games he loved cricket the most. He judged everything and everyone by the game. The only time I ever saw him lost for words was when someone confessed they neither knew nor cared about cricket. Then he would shake his head sadly baffled that a great part of his world – for cricket was surely that – could mean so little to any other sane human being. Last season a friend and I took him to Headingley and sat him behind the bowler's arm and he never moved all day. We brought him pork pies and sandwiches and good Yorkshire beer, and he sat under his native sun watching Lillee bowl fast and he was the happiest man on our planet.

You always knew where my old man would be on any cricket ground: right behind the bowler's arm. Moreover, if ever you lost him, or he lost himself as he often did, being born without a sense of direction – you simply asked the whereabouts of the nearest cricket ground and there you would discover the old man sitting contentedly awaiting the arrival of his search party.

When he finished playing he took up coaching, first the local youngsters and latterly his three grandchildren. They, like me, are left-handed batsmen. Not because God made them so, but because the old man's theory was that not many players like bowling at left-handers. His other theory, based on a lifetime's experience, was that fast bowlers are crazy, so he determined to make at least one of my sons a slow bowler.

The consequence of this is that I once had the only eight-year-old googly bowler in the Western Hemisphere. At ten he added the top spinner to his repertoire and when he was twelve the old man's face was a picture as his protégé beat me with a googly and then had me plumb in front of the dustbin with one that hurried off the pitch and came straight through. The old man's name was John William, and he hated John Willy. If anyone addressed him thus when he was playing in his prime, the red alert went up and the casualty ward at Barnsley Beckett Hospital could look forward to receiving visitors.

He's been dead a long time now, but I still think about him because he was a special man and I was lucky to know him. He was a Yorkshireman, a miner, a humorist and a fast bowler. Not a bad combination.

I only hope they play cricket in heaven. If they don't, he'll ask for a transfer.

John Major

THE RT HON. JOHN MAJOR MP once said that his vision of England included cricket on the village green with warm beer, and he is a keen follower of both cricket and football. He also shares a love of opera with his wife Norma; they have a daughter and a son. He has been MP for Huntingdon since 1983 and was Prime Minister from 1990 to 1997.

Meanwhile, other great cricketing fans were growing up around Britain, unaware of what life had in store for them ...

HOUSE OF COMMONS
LONDON SW1A 0AA

FROM THE RT. HON. JOHN MAJOR, MP

My mother had a great gift for lame ducks. All her
life she seemed to attract them, much to the amuse-
ment of her family, and sometimes, at the frustration of her neighbours.

I remember, as a boy, a gypsy knocking at our door
in Worcester Park who looked as though he had not
eaten for some time – or at least so my mother
thought. He was whisked into the kitchen, sat down
and presented with *my* lunch, which he thoroughly
enjoyed.

I didn't begrudge him this, since I rather felt that an
alternative lunch would be provided. But somehow
my mother overlooked this.

As he left the gypsy warmly thanked my mother. I
have always thought he might have offered some
thanks to me, as well. But, alas, he did not.

John Major

Jeffrey Archer

JEFFREY ARCHER (Lord Archer of Weston-super-Mare) was
born on 15 April 1940 and has had a varied career as a politician and author of numerous bestselling novels. His wife is
the noted scientist Dr Mary Archer; they live at the Old
Vicarage, Grantchester, on the outskirts of Cambridge, made
famous by Rupert Brooke's poem, and have two sons. He lists
his recreations as the theatre, watching Somerset play cricket,
and acting as an amateur auctioneer.

*In all cultures, grandmothers have played a central role in
family life. As a prelude to our next story, here's one nine-
year-old's definition of a grandma ...*

Grandmothers don't have to do anything except to be
there. If they take us for walks they slow down past
things like pretty leaves and caterpillars, and they
never say "hurry up".

Usually grandmothers are fat but not too fat to tie
your shoes. They wear glasses and funny underwear
and they can take their teeth and gums out.

Grandmothers don't have to be clever, just be able
to answer questions like "Why isn't God married?" and
"Why do dogs chase cats?"

Grandmothers don't talk baby talk to us like
visitors do because they know it's hard for us to understand it.

When they read to us, they don't skip pages.

Or mind if it's the same story over and over again.

Everybody should have a grandmother especially if
you don't have television ... because they're the only
grown ups that have time.

*Jeffrey Archer remembers his grandmother – with very good
reason!*

As a schoolboy, one of my more memorable
experiences is of a journey I took during a school
holiday, from Weston-super-Mare in Somerset to
Leeds in Yorkshire. The purpose of the journey was to
spend Christmas with an aunt and uncle who were
school teachers in North Allerton and as I had never
before travelled beyond Bristol or Bridgwater, I
looked forward to the day with much anticipation and
relish. My grandmother was one of those early drivers
who had not acquired a licence, and had she ever
taken the test she would have undoubtedly frightened
the examiner out of his wits.

We left Weston-super-Mare in the morning in a large green Morris Oxford. My grandmother drove, my grandfather and mother in the back, while I had the honour of sitting in the front, decades before anyone had thought of seatbelts. My grandmother, like myself, rarely travelled beyond the environs of Weston-super-Mare and for her the roundabout was a new-fangled invention which she had not encountered before. We discovered the first one some seven miles outside my home town, over which she happily drove straight across the middle and carried on in a northerly direction. We encountered twenty-three such obstacles set unnecessarily in our progress, on our route between Weston-super-Mare and Leeds and my grandmother crossed all of them in a manner which would have pleased Hannibal.

On arrival in Leeds, my grandfather who had learnt several years before not to speak, my mother who was not listened to when she did, and I who did not murmur a word, breathed more than a sigh of relief when we eventually arrived at my uncle's front door in one piece. Once safely on the premises, I ventured the innocent question of my grandmother, "Surely one should go around roundabouts and not across them?" She replied with British certainty, "Certainly not. What you must understand, young man, is that they will never catch on", a degree of logic with which I am still quite unable to find fault.

We returned home by train.

Ann Widdecombe

THE RT HON. ANN WIDDECOMBE MP has been MP for Maidstone since 1987. Born on 4 October 1947, her father James was a leading naval administrator. Educated at the University of Birmingham and Lady Margaret Hall, Oxford, her hobbies include researching the escape of Charles II after the Battle of Worcester.

ONE of the most testing times for any family is separation, particularly where younger members of the family are involved. In 1953, when I was not yet six and my brother not yet sixteen, my father was posted to Singapore. My brother was left behind, in the tradition of the time, at boarding school but because, in those days, there was no assistance given for children to travel out from boarding school in the school holidays my brother stayed in England for the whole three years in which we were in Singapore. Not only did we have to leave my brother behind but we also left behind my grandmother who had been living with us.

Only now can I realise how dreadful it must have been for my mother and indeed the others. Fortunately I was too young to appreciate the reality of the separation and so when I returned to England I not only had the excitement of a new country but of two sudden additions to the family as well, whom, because of my age, I had almost forgotten! The day that we were all assembled again around Sunday lunch, my parents, my grandmother, my brother and myself was a wonderful occasion. It was not long before we added a cat and a dog.

Tony Blair

THE RT. HON TONY BLAIR MP was born on 6 May 1953 and practised as a lawyer specialising in employment and industrial
law before entering Parliament in June 1983 as MP for
Sedgefield. In 1994 he was elected Leader of the Labour Party
and in May 1997 became Prime Minister. He married another
lawyer, Cherie Booth, now a barrister and Queen's Counsel,
in 1980 and they have two sons and a daughter.

*The Prime Minister, Tony Blair, had a very international
childhood. Like Ann Widdecombe, he found that travelling
long distances as a child brought its own bewildering
surprises.*

10 DOWNING STREET
LONDON SW1A 2AA

THE PRIME MINISTER

I always think that Christmas is a special time for children. One of my earliest childhood memories is of my final Christmas in Australia where we lived while my father was lecturing at the University of Adelaide. My family's return to England meant that there would be no more Christmas afternoon walks down to the beach to eat ice-cream. The traditional image of Christmas, with its snow-covered roof-tops and Santa Claus dressed in a large red coat must have made little sense to me. I was soon to find out that Christmas in County Durham would be no less enjoyable and the scenery no less beautiful, but it was certainly different.

Tony Blair

Colin Dexter

COLIN DEXTER was born on 29 September 1930 in Lincolnshire, where he grew up. After a career as a classics teacher, he began writing and the first of his famous 'Inspector Morse' stories was published in 1975. He lives in Oxford, the setting for most of the Morse books and of the television series.

Emotional blackmail – from the parents of a murder-mystery writer ...

M Y chief memory of family life in Stamford, Lincolnshire, is of my brother, my sister, and myself, in our dining-room (and everything-else-ing-room) sitting around the table doing homework. Both parents had left school at the age of twelve, and their attitude was predictable: "You've got the chance we never had. Make the most of it!"

So we did.

It was bordering on emotional blackmail, I suppose, but we were very happy with the arrangement because we were never expected to perform those chores which are the causes of civil wars in most families: washing up; emptying chamber-pots; cleaning shoes; making beds; tidying up; peeling potatoes.

Carol Vorderman

CAROL VORDERMAN was born on Christmas Eve 1960. She grew up in North Wales and studied engineering at Cambridge before becoming the resident statistician on Channel 4's *Countdown*. Since then she has gone on to appear on many science-based or educational programmes on television, including *Tomorrow's World*.

"... we were poor, we were happy and very close."

*E*VEN though we were poor, we were happy and very close. Mum was adamant that my brother Anton, sister Trixie and I should always be able to earn a living. And, before each child was nine, she'd taught us to touch-type and take Pitman's short-hand.

Our lessons were hilarious. Mum would put on an old "78" record of the "William Tell Overture" and off I'd go on a rickety old manual typewriter. They were fun times. To this day, I still hear the sound of the "William Tell Overture" every time I use a keyboard!

David Puttnam

LORD DAVID PUTTNAM, one of Britain's best-known film producers (*Bugsy Malone*, *Chariots of Fire* and *The Killing Fields*, among many others), was born on 25 February 1941 to Leonard and Marie. He married Patricia in 1961 and they have a son and a daughter. He was made a Life Peer in 1997.

Even when life is filled with successes, the earliest ones are still strong in the memory ...

$\mathcal{S}$ATURDAY, I remember it was a Saturday, and being woken up by this sort of scream at home, and then hearing my mother racing upstairs crashing into the bedroom, jumping on the bed and hugging me, "You passed, you passed, you passed." I'd forgotten it was the day of the eleven-plus results, and I realise now looking back what an incredible thing this was to her and, to an extent, to my dad.

I hadn't thought about this before, but the implications of failure for the people who on that same morning got letters saying they hadn't done it, were with hindsight devastating – really devastating.

Patrick Moore

PATRICK MOORE CBE was born on 4 March 1923 and educated at home due to illness. After serving with the RAF in the Second World War, he went on to become one of Britain's most popular astronomers, having appeared in BBC TV's *The Sky at Night* since 1957, made numerous broadcasts and written many books. He lists as his recreations cricket, chess, tennis, music (including composing) and playing the xylophone.

We came across a poem which suggests that children can be less than generous ...

A TODDLER'S PROPERTY LAWS

If I like it, it's mine.

If it's in my hand, it's mine.

If I can take it from you, it's mine.

If we're building something, all the pieces are mine.

If it's mine, it must never ever in any way appear to be
     yours.

If I saw it first, it's mine.

If it looks like mine, it's mine.

If you're playing with something and you put it down,
     it automatically becomes mine.

If it's broken, it's yours.

It's true that kids can be selfish but they can also be open-handed in a way that's all the more endearing for its spontaneity. We're sure that this mum and dad never forgot an all-expenses paid holiday funded by a certain budding astronomer ...

Dr. Patrick Moore, CBE, FRAS

When I was aged 12½, I decided to spend my 6d pocket money on football pools. My mother had to sign the coupon, and we had an agreement that any winnings would be split.

Suddenly - we won £87! A fortune! I had £43 in my pocket. I said 'Right. On this, we're all going on a holiday to Belgium.' We did. My £43 paid for travel, hotel at Heyst-sur-Mur and outings. The lot ..... A great 'family occasion'.

I have never won a penny since!

Patrick Moore

David Alton

DAVID ALTON (Lord Alton of Liverpool) was MP for
Liverpool constituencies from 1979 to 1997, after becoming
the city's – and Britain's – youngest City Councillor in 1972.
Born on 15 March 1951 to Frederick and Bridget, he married
Dilys in 1988 and they have three sons and a daughter. A com-
mitted Christian, he writes books and articles on both
Christianity and politics.

*T*HE first thing the Bible says after describing
creation is that "it is not good for man to be
alone". But, as Adam and Eve and Cain and Abel
soon discovered, if it is not good to be alone, it is
even more difficult to live together!

For me, the strength of the extended family, with
its network of aunts and uncles, grandmothers and
grandfathers – the supporting cast who keep the
show on the road – is usually to be found in
moments of uncertainty and moments of crisis.

The strength of the family is especially important
at times of death. Three years ago my father died –
and just before Christmas my mother died after a
long, crippling illness.

When they had married, nearly fifty years before, my father had just been demobbed. He served as a Desert Rat in the Eighth Army. His younger brother, Ted, who had been in the RAF, had been killed. Their family home in the East End of London had been blitzed. My mother was an Irish speaker from the west of Ireland. Her family were survivors of the Highland Clearances and the Irish Famine. She had fallen in love with my father and not long after they married.

They married across the denominational divide – with all that implied in those days. Not long after, my mother's younger sister, another Irish Catholic, married an Ulster Protestant. Ultimately, the family came to terms with what for many was an unthinkable taboo.

Fifty years later, in the same church where the wedding of my parents had taken place, where I had been confirmed, and where my sister had made her first communion, my father's funeral was held. It was conducted by my father-in-law, an Anglican priest, and held in a Catholic church. My Northern Irish uncle told me that he felt many blessings from the service. Families can sometimes accommodate what prejudice would never allow.

My Family

As a child I was given a jigsaw puzzle. On one side was the picture of a man. On the other side was a picture of the world. It was virtually impossible for a child to get the world right but the great thing about the jigsaw puzzle was that if you got the man right, and turned the jigsaw over, the world came right anyway.

In the context of the Northern Ireland peace process, and the continued sectarian enmities, I can't help thinking that it is in the context of our families that we can get the bigger picture right too.

Michael Palin

MICHAEL PALIN is a writer and actor who made his name
with *Monty Python's Flying Circus*, and has become widely
known more recently for his travel programmes on television
and the books which accompany them. He has also written
three books for children. The son of Edward and Mary, he
was born on 5 May 1943 and married Helen in 1966; they have
two sons and a daughter. He lists his recreations as reading,
running and railways – preferably all three in a foreign
country.

*Growing up in a family means that you cannot choose the
people you live with. Perhaps learning to live with them, no
matter who they are, is one of the most important lessons life
has to teach us. It can also be the cause of some drama ...*

*A*MONG the few things that really united our
family – my father, mother and my sister
Angela – were arrivals, departures and a love of cats.
I remember one afternoon when all three came
together at virtually the same time. My sister had
arrived from London on the lunchtime train. Angela
was nine years older than me and I was very proud

of the fact that she worked for an architect at some flashy Sloane Square address in London while I was still stuck in Sheffield. I didn't let on I was proud of her, that would have been very sissy. But I was, and still am, though she died more than ten years ago. Anyway, it was school holidays and my father had taken me with him to the station to meet her off the Thames–Clyde Express. I was very chuffed, because though I loved seeing my sister, I loved seeing trains even more.

It was on time, which was hugely rare, Angela was in a good mood, the sun was shining (I made that bit up, but I feel it must have been true), and we were all terribly pleased to see each other. An added excitement was that my older cousin Hank, a darkly handsome, laconic Australian had been staying with us and had delayed his departure in order to meet Angela. I was a bit nervous as to how she might react to him, as he was a bit of a wild boy who cared very little for English social niceties and my parents had found him quite a handful.

I needn't have worried. He was at his most charming and Angela at her most accommodating. She even seemed to forget all about the telephone, for which she usually made a bee-line within five minutes of arriving home. It was one of those rare and

wonderful moments of family harmony as we all sat
around chatting and drinking tea (or coffee for my
Sloaney sister, of course). That is, until it was Hank's
turn to leave. Suddenly there was a minor crisis.
Jezebel the cat had gone missing.

My father, who was particularly fond of her, was
quite distraught.

"He can't go without saying goodbye to Jezebel!"

But there was no sign of her in all the usual
places, and we were soon despatched far and wide.
My father ran into the garden and I later saw him
out on the road, looking fearfully one way and then
the other.

The only one who didn't join in this cat hunt was
Hank, who stood, quite unconcerned, in the hallway,
until, having judged the search to have reached
panic stage (I think my mother was actually phoning
the neighbours), he shouted out to us, in exactly the
right note of incredulous surprise, "Oh, *here* she is!"

And with that he reached inside his long black
coat, pulled out Jezebel and held her aloft by the
scruff of the neck. No one had picked up Jezebel in
this unceremonious fashion since her mother had
carried her out of the box she was born in, and she
wore a pitiable, frozen, Job-like look of sufferance, as
she dangled high above the hall table.

My Family

My mother screamed, my father swore and
Angela went off to make a telephone call.

For me it was a defining moment. I had never
quite understood what made Australians different
from us. Now I knew. And I was secretly awfully
glad that Hank, too, was one of our family.

Kenny Dalglish

KENNY DALGLISH MBE was born on 4 March 1951 and became a professional footballer in 1970. From 1977 he played for Liverpool and was the club's manager from 1985 to 1991. He is the only player to have scored more than 100 goals in both the English and Scottish Leagues, and was capped a record 102 times for Scotland in football internationals, scoring a joint record total of 30 goals. He was manager of Newcastle United until August 1998.

> I put my hand over hers and told her ... quite seriously, not to get too attached to the little thing, because she couldn't keep him. I did this to spare her from what I had seen happen to other women ... who were nearly destroyed by the discovery that purely and simply children are crops. One raises them and they go away.
>
> — *Preston Sturges, Sr. on the birth of his son:*
> *from* Preston Sturges *by Preston Sturges.*

When Kenny Dalglish's secretary told us a contribution was on the way we waited eagerly to see what memory would be special to this footballing genius. When Kenny's contribution came it was simple and yet deeply moving and took us back to those days when our own children came into the world.

*T*HERE have been four special memories in my life that I would like to share with you. They are the births of my four children, Kelly, Paul, Lynsey and Lauren, each occasion as special and memorable as the other.

My wife Marina and I are exceptionally proud of our children who are as special to us now as the day they were born.

Dickie Bird

DICKIE BIRD MBE was born Harold Dennis Bird on 19 April 1933 to James and Ethel. A famous and highly-respected cricket umpire, from 1970 to 1996 he was an international umpire for Test cricket, and has written several books on the sport, including his autobiography.

TWELVE SONGS IX

Stop all the clocks, cut off the telephone,
Prevent the dog from barking with a juicy bone,
Silence the pianos and with muffled drum
Bring out the coffin, let the mourners come.

Let aeroplanes circle moaning overhead
Scribbling on the sky the message He Is Dead.
Put crepe bows round the white necks of public doves,
Let the traffic policemen wear black cotton gloves.

He was my North, my South, my East and West.
My working week and my Sunday rest,
My noon, my midnight, my talk, my song;
I thought that love would last forever; I was wrong.

My Family

> The stars are not wanted now: put out every one;
> Pack up the moon and dismantle the sun;
> Pour away the ocean and sweep up the wood;
> For nothing now can ever come to any good.

> – *W. H. Auden*

ONE of the saddest memories of my life was the death of my sister at the age of forty-one. She died from a brain haemorrhage and this was a very traumatic time for my mother, my younger sister and myself.

Fiona Castle

FIONA CASTLE was born in West Kirby, the youngest of four children born to her GP father and mother. At the age of nine, following in the footsteps of her ballroom-dancing mother, Fiona showed a talent for ballet and was sent to a full-time dancing school in Surrey. After taking her O levels, Fiona concentrated entirely on dance, drama and stagecraft. While she was appearing in *The Sound of Music*, a mutual friend, Eric Morecambe, introduced her to Roy Castle. They eventually married in 1963 and had four children. In 1994, after thirty-one years of marriage, Roy lost his fight again lung cancer. Since his death Fiona continues to work with The Roy Castle Cause for Hope Foundation, raising funds to build the world's first lung cancer research centre. She is the author of *Give Us This Day* and *No Flowers ... Just Lots of Joy*, and compiler of *Rainbow through the Rain*.

Recently a friend commented to me that many people live their life as though it were a dress rehearsal for the real thing. But in fact, by tonight we will have given the only performance of "today" that we will ever give. So we have to put all our heart, our energy and honesty and sincerity into what we do every day. As a show business family, we find that a very suitable illustration. And every show comes to the end of its run, when we must lay aside the costumes and step off the stage, into another, larger world.

– from Give Us This Day *by Fiona Castle,*
written while Roy was battling against cancer

*I*F I'd ever needed hope and assurance for the future, Roy produced it for me just days before he died. He had such a strong belief in heaven. He described a most beautiful garden that he saw himself standing in. He told me it was difficult to describe because it was more beautiful than anything he had seen on earth.

"I thought I was a gardener," he said, "but this gardener's something else." It must have been pretty good, because he said, "Darling, I want you to see it – don't hang around."

Fiona's next memory illustrates the universal law that if kids can possibly drop you in it – they will!

O N the first day of a new school term the teacher used to send home a letter to every parent. It read, "If you promise not to believe everything your child tells you goes on at school, then I promise not to believe all they tell me goes on at home."

At the age of five, my youngest son Ben was invited to a football match at Wembley with a school friend and his mother.

The next day I panicked because I hadn't bought a present so that Ben could say thank you. A box of chocolates was produced from the cupboard, hurriedly wrapped and Ben went happily off to school. Later that day when I had collected Ben from school, the phone rang and before I could get to it, Ben had picked it up. After a few moments, to my horror, I heard him saying, "Oh don't worry. We didn't have to pay for them – they were some we had left over from Christmas"!

Sally Gunnell

SALLY GUNNELL MBE was born on 29 July 1966 and won the
400 metres hurdles at the Olympic Games in 1992. She has
also been World Champion (1992), European Champion
(1994) and Commonwealth Champion (1994) and held the
world record for the distance in 1993. She was Commonwealth champion for the 100 metres hurdles in 1986 and 1990
and captained the British Athletics Team from 1992 to 1997. In
1992 she married Jonathan Bigg and retired from competition
in 1997.

*I*T'S known as "the turkey episode" in the Bigg
family! I met my husband Jon during the summer
of 1986, and he is the middle of three brothers. At
that time Chris, the eldest, was at art college and
Matt, the youngest, was attending sixth form. We all
got along very well and I was invited to spend
Christmas Day with the family in Brighton and it
was my idea to have a fancy dress competition with
Jon's mum and dad as judges.

I knew exactly what I would wear. My father sup-
plied turkeys and during plucking time I was to be
found in the shed selecting only the very best feathers. These I sewed onto a long-sleeved leotard with

the longest along the sleeves to form wings, and with flesh coloured tights, a white swim cap and a cardboard beak, there I was - a turkey!

During the run-up to Christmas the Bigg boys tried to get out of me what I would be wearing but there was no way I was going to tell them. Christmas Day arrived and I packed my outfit in a very large bag and headed off to Brighton.

After the usual large Christmas lunch I suggested that now was the time for the parade. So off the four of us went to change. After a long struggle I was ready to make my appearance. Down the stairs I went – frightening Jon's cat on the way – into the lounge, only to find those Bigg boys still in their ordinary clothes, rolled up with laughter. They had had no intention of dressing up and had strung me along all the time. And there I was completely encased in feathers!

I have gradually got my own back on them. How? Well, that would be another story!

Frank Bruno

FRANK BRUNO MBE was born to Robert and Lynette on 16 November 1961. As a professional boxer he has fought forty-five contests and won forty of them, including becoming European Heavyweight Champion 1985-86 and WBC World Heavyweight Champion in 1995. He also appears regularly in pantomime. In 1990 he married Laura and they have a son and two daughters.

"... more nervous than if I was facing Mike Tyson"

*T*HE most memorable day in our lives came when we finally tied the knot ...

Nicola and Rachel were bridesmaids, along with Laura's sister Jane, Jane's daughter Louise and my niece Michelle. I know that everybody thinks that their wedding day is special, but this one stood out as if it was blessed from up above. Father McSweeney told the congregation: "Frank and Laura have come here today to make what amounts to a public statement that they intend to spend the rest of their lives together."

A choir of fifty school children led us through

"All things bright and beautiful" and "Morning has broken" and Laura and I listened with tears in our eyes as Father McSweeney quoted the Good Book: "without love, I have nothing at all".

The speeches by best man Michael and Laura's father were excellent and mine seemed to go down all right despite me being more nervous than if I was facing Mike Tyson. Harry made a moving and humorous speech and Terry amused us all by presenting me with a box of Kleenex and a bottle of HP sauce – two products with which I have been happy to have been associated.

Then the show was stolen by my mum, who brought just about everybody to tears with what was almost a sermon. I think that everybody suddenly realised that I have a mum in a million, and if I ever get half as good as her at expressing myself I shall be able to hold the attention of any audience.

Ian McCaskill

IAN MCCASKILL's unmistakable voice has been forecasting the weather on BBC TV and radio since 1978. Born in Glasgow on 28 July 1938, he is married to Pat and has two daughters.

Ian McCaskill recently got married too ...

*T*HE last time my extended family were together was in May. At my wedding. (We decided to give the babbies a name!) Being Scottish we had to make economies and hired a huge marquee, but baulked at the cost of portable loos. The house loos managed fine, but the septic tank didn't. We had to go round the guests blaming the farmer for spraying the field. God forgive us! He did at least send us the greenest grass in Yorkshire the following week. And we are still married!

Lynda Lee-Potter

LYNDA LEE-POTTER began her career as a successful actress
and is now a columnist and feature writer for the *Daily Mail*.
In 1957 she married Jeremy, a leading haematologist, and they
have two daughters and a son, all of whom are journalists.

*Families are fine, and weddings are wonderful, but when
you put the two together anything can happen. Lynda Lee-
Potter experienced some of the joy when her daughter got
married.*

THE marquee is being erected, the grass is newly
mown and every morning I say, "Please God let
there be scorching sun on Saturday when my
daughter gets married". Everything that can be
fixed has been fixed including ten barrow-loads of
plants put in the garden on Bank Holiday Monday,
but, unfortunately, I have no control over the
Almighty.

In her book about how to run the perfect party,
Lady Anson of Party Planners says that when
you're organising a wedding it's vital to decide how
much you want to spend and stick to it, which is

wise, wonderful and shrewd advice we've been foolish enough to ignore.

The champagne is now well stocked in the larder and I've replaced the odd bottle I purloined when I was having a nervous crisis. The bride's frock is hanging in the spare room covered in tissue paper and the bridesmaid is still making hers to the anguished implorations of the bride's mother screaming, "Will you get a move on? The one thing I can't stand is you being driven to the church still sewing bits of your frock!"

This, I may add is the usual way she goes to parties so it's not a needless worry, as though I haven't got worries enough, including the guest list, which is like everyone else's guest list. There are those you want to show off, the ones you'd like to put in a corner with a cloth over their heads, the ones you pray won't meet your boss and those whose behaviour is unpredictable after a few glasses of champagne, including my father and me who get tearful and sentimental when we've had a few.

When I got married my mother was so determined my left-wing grandad wouldn't stand up in the middle of the reception to denounce the medical profession and the upper middle classes, both of which he despised and which I was marrying into, she put sleeping pills into his breakfast tea.

All my friends have got new outfits for the day and I've got a Jean Muir suit plus lethally high shoes on account of the bridegroom's mother having stunning legs, and one doesn't want to be overshadowed does one?

I've got a wonderfully grand hat and I've been practising wearing that as well, having read yet another book on wedding etiquette which says bossily "the family must feel at home in their clothes".

Yesterday I met a rather amazed neighbour as I walked up and down the drive in wellies, jeans, an old jumper and cream hat trimmed with ostrich feathers. "It's a bit fancy isn't it?" said my auntie critically. "Well after all," I said grandly, "I *am* the mother of the bride."

On the day we're having what in Lancashire we used to call "a sit down do" on account of the fact that I can think of nothing worse than trying to juggle a plate, fork, glass and then stand through what I hope will be brilliantly witty speeches.

The bride and I rarely quarrel but last week we had such a humdinger that when a friend said, "What are you going to throw at her as she leaves church?" I could only think of bricks. My favourite joke at the moment is the one about the guest who says to the person he finds himself standing next to in the marquee, "Are you a friend of the bride-groom?" "Certainly not," she snarls, "I'm the bride's mother." This I may say in our case is far from the truth on account of the fact that we think the groom is so lovely we keep saying to the bride, "Oh, aren't you lucky?"

This however is more flattering than what my mother said to me when I took my very good-looking husband-to-be home all those years ago. "I don't know what he sees in you love", she said. "I think he could have done better for himself."

William Hague

THE RT HON. WILLIAM HAGUE MP has been involved in
Conservative politics since his schooldays, when he attracted
attention by addressing the Conservative Party Conference
in 1977. Born on 26 March 1961 to Timothy and Stella, he has
been MP for Richmond in Yorkshire since 1986 and became
Leader of the Conservative Party in June 1997. In the same
year he married his Welsh wife Ffion in the chapel of the
Houses of Parliament.

I grew up in Rotherham in a very close-knit family. With my mum and dad, and my three sisters, we did almost everything together. And in one way or another we all worked for the family company – Hague Soft Drinks. We had various home brands like Hague Cola, Hague Cherryade and, my favourite, Hague Dandelion and Burdock. I still have some of the old bottles in my kitchen at home in Catterick, North Yorkshire.

The firm also used to supply beer and spirits to the working men's clubs of South Yorkshire. During the school holidays, my job was to help deliver beer to the clubs in Rotherham. We'd begin at eight o'clock in the morning. Our truck would pull up at the first club, and the driver and I would off-load these huge kegs of beer and get them into the cellar.

It was thirsty work. At the end of the first delivery, the club owner would give us a pint each for our efforts. And so it went on through the day. One club would follow another. I'd lose count of the number of kegs I'd wheeled along the pavement or heaved down into the cellar. And I would soon lose track of the number of pints I'd downed. By the end of the day I'd feel decidedly the worse for wear – though, as a proud young man, I'd fiercely deny I was drunk.

Staggering home in the evening I'd get a little ticking off from my mother. But I don't think she really meant it – after all, it was all in the line of duty.

The Rt Hon. William Hague MP

Jilly Cooper

JILLY COOPER was born on 21 February 1937 and married Leo in 1961; they have a daughter and a son. A prolific and best-selling author, she lists her recreations as merry-making, wild flowers, music and mongrels.

Listen, I can be president of the United States, or I can control Alice. I cannot possibly do both.

— President Theodore Roosevelt of his oldest daughter

A hassled mother once said, "Insanity is hereditary; you get it from your kids." It may be true, but there are usually some laughs on the way to madness, as Jilly's story relates.

This is a story I included in my book *The Common Years*, published by Corgi Books. I was walking with the children one Sunday when I suppose they were about six and nine or perhaps five and eight, and they had a long discussion about how old I'll be when they're both seventy, which went as follows:

Emily says: "You'll be over a hundred, mummy, and paralysed, and you'll have lost all your legs and arms."

Felix says: "You might not, if you use Oil of Ulay."

Felix then says he loves me more than anything else in the world, then on reflection adds truthfully: "Except television."

I feel this is a *very* high compliment.

Love

Jilly Coop

Jilly Cooper

Pam Rhodes

PAM RHODES lives in Hertfordshire with her two children.
Trained both as a dancer and a youth worker, she has presented the BBC's *Songs of Praise* for more than ten years, which
has involved interviewing many people who have found faith
during traumatic times in their lives.

*Families are sometimes places of broken dreams. When couples
split, the pain is often excruciating, not least for children. Life
goes on however, and so do families, finding new ways of
being together. Pam Rhodes has courageously shared the pain
she went through in the following story.*

*J*UST over three years ago, my family became a
statistic in a way I could never previously have
imagined. The husband I had been happily married
to for fifteen years left me for a woman fifteen years
younger than me, so that it felt as if all our years
together had been wiped out as irrelevant.

Our son, Max, was just twelve at the time, and
our daughter, Bethan, almost six. I suppose we all
went into a kind of panic – especially me, as I strug-
gled not just with an overwhelming sense of failure,

rejection and guilt, but also with the daunting prospect of bringing up two wonderful children on my own.

I've spent years talking to people on *Songs of Praise* about how their faith has helped them through traumatic times in their lives, and yet I have to admit that during that first month, it felt as if my prayers were going nowhere. If God was listening, He was keeping His distance. The loneliness of that time was unbearable.

But finally, I got myself together enough to realise that the only way forward for us as a family was for me to start taking control, and to make practical decisions about our home and the finances. And it was then, when I began to be pro-active, rather than merely re-active, that I became aware of feeling I was gently cupped in God's hand. I saw it in the most down-to-earth ways – in the buyer who turned up at just the right time to buy our home, in the wonderful house we found that was perfect for us; in the neighbours who turned up with pots of paint and casseroles; in the wonderful friends who were endlessly patient in allowing me to blub all over them. Most of all, I saw it in my children. In our confusion, we clung together, and the depth of love we've found in each other is just wonderful. Sometimes it's felt as if it's "us" against "the world" – and that bond of unity has grown and flourished so that we really value each other. "I love you" are words that are said very often between the three of us. And in spite of everything that's happened, I look at them, and count my blessings.

Richard Madeley
and Judy Finnigan

RICHARD MADELEY and JUDY FINNIGAN are the husband and wife team who have presented ITV's *This Morning* programme since 1988. They have four children, two together and twin boys from Judy's first marriage.

> I remember imagining that the egg-timer held not
> sand but the years of our children's lives. The first
> eighteen contain 6,570 days. If your daughter is ten
> years old you have 2,920 left. So far as is possible in
> this busy world, try not to miss one of them.
>
> – *from* The Sixty Minute Father *by Rob Parsons*

One of the pleasures you do not want to miss is children's inexorable logic ...

Granada Television
Franciscan Court
16 Hatfields, London SE1 8DJ
TEL: 0171-620 1620 FAX: 0171-578 4121/4122

It was the day before Hallowe'en, and we were driving our two youngest children, Jack and Chloe, then aged five and four, back from infant school.

We passed a fancy dress shop and asked the children what they wanted to wear when we took them trick-or-treating the following night.

Jack, whose reply has not varied for six years now, said: "Dracula."

Chloe answered: "A peanut." Mystified, we asked her why. She explained that at a summer fancy dress party a friend had come dressed in a huge fake packet of KP peanuts, which had driven her to depths of envy her young soul had not experienced before.

We pointed out that although it was a lovely costume, Hallowe'en fancy dress was meant to be scary. There followed a long silence as Chloe ruminated. Then she said: "All right; I'll come as a nasty peanut then. "

We nearly drove off the road and were incapable of coherent speech for several hours.

Richard Madeley and Judy Finnigan

Jane Asher

JANE ASHER is the daughter of a doctor and was born on 5 April 1946. A very successful actress on stage, film and television, she also won the Radio Actress of the Year Award in 1986. A renowned cake-maker, she writes books on children's issues and cookery and is concerned with several children's charities, including as President of the National Autistic Society. She is married to Gerald Scarfe and they have two sons and a daughter.

*I*T's always a proud and moving moment to watch your little darling in a school concert or play. One of my favourites was when the headmistress of my five-year-old son's school was sent to find me in the middle of the nativity play. She brought the urgent message that "one of the three Kings wants his mummy". After a quick cuddle His Royal Highness was able to go on and gave a very noble performance and carried his frankincense without incident. He's now sixteen and six foot two, but still, I'm glad to say, needs his mummy from time to time.

Harry Secombe

SIR HARRY SECOMBE was born on 8 September 1921 and grew up in Swansea. During the Second World War he served in the Royal Artillery but has worked as a singer, actor and comedian since 1948. Still affectionately remembered for his role in the *Goon Show*, he presented TV's *Highway* from 1983 to 1993. He married Myra in 1948 and they have two sons and two daughters.

I had just returned from a trip to New York and went upstairs for a rest after an arduous flight. It was afternoon time in England but I was five hours behind in my body clock.

At about six o'clock, Myra asked Katy, our four-year-old daughter, to go upstairs and see if I was awake.

She came upstairs to our bedroom, took a long look at my sleeping form, went back down the stairs to her mother and reported without a twinge of sorrow: "I fink he's dead."

Another time, her mother had reprimanded her for not cleaning her teeth, saying, "Even if you pretend to have brushed them, God will know that you have not."

The following morning, after much splashing and spluttering, Katy emerged from the bathroom and to the landing. Lifting her head to the heavens she declared: "Look God, I've cleaned 'em."

Not surprisingly she is now an actress.

Alex Ferguson

ALEX FERGUSON CBE, manager of Manchester United Football Club since 1986, was born on 31 December 1941. A professional football player, he moved into management in 1974. In 1966 he married Catherine and they have three sons.

"You always hurt the one you love." Well it turned out to be true for one of the most successful football managers of all time.

*T*HE year 1983 was particularly special for me. I was managing Aberdeen Football Club and we had just beaten Real Madrid in the European Cup Winners Cup in Gothenburg. It was the end of a wonderful season and the family and I were looking forward to our first trip to Disneyland. Never having been before we were a little unsure of what to expect, but through a dear friend, Harold Bell, who put together the three-week package, off we set.

On arrival in the States, we piled into the car and set off to find the hotel. Well! With having to cope with driving on the wrong side of the road, and three excited children, plus getting lost, and having to stop to ask the way, we finally arrived late in the afternoon.

As we drove into the car park at the hotel there was a big sign in big neon lights saying, "Circus World welcomes Alex Ferguson and family". I doubt anyone in America had ever even heard of Alex Ferguson. Our dear friend Harold had obviously organised it and the kids thought it was great. "Dad, you must be famous", they kept saying.

Then, just as we were taking our cases out of the car, one of those famous Florida thunder-storms broke, sending the rain down in torrents and the family running for cover. It was only when we were under cover and doing a head count we turned to see Jason standing behind the car, his little legs going ten to the dozen like a cartoon character, that we realised we had a problem.

I ran back to the car only to find he had trapped his fingers in the boot. As I was unlocking the boot and dreading to look in case I had to pick up individual fingers, he let out a scream and was obviously in pain.

Thankfully the hotel staff were wonderful and directed us to the emergency room at the local hospital. Fortunately there were no bones broken, and Jason's hand was only bruised – but what a start to a holiday!

Diane Louise Jordan

DIANE LOUISE JORDAN was born in 1959 and had a successful career as an actress before becoming one of the presenters of BBC's *Blue Peter* in 1989. Her huge appeal has led her into a variety of roles since she left *Blue Peter* in 1996, including an invitation in 1997 to sit on the Diana, Princess of Wales Memorial Fund Committee.

A ninety-five-year-old woman once came into Rob Parsons'
law office and declared, "I can rest in peace now, my son."
"Why is that?" asked Rob.
"I've just got my youngest into an old people's home."
She wasn't in a home herself, but her son was in his early
seventies and had become a bit shaky.
Parenting is for the long term, and the worry doesn't stop
just because you can't do anything to help. Perhaps the most
difficult time of all is when your children are teenagers ...

WHEN my daughter, Justine, was a toddler we did everything together – shopped, read bed-time stories, visited the park. I was there for nappy changing, stayed up on the stomach-achy sleepless nights and collected her from school.

These days – with Justine on the brink of teenage years – I rarely read her a bedtime story. She prefers to snuggle up under the duvet engrossed in the latest *Point Horror* thriller. Illuminations courtesy of torch light and ambience created by the faint drones of Capital Radio. The prominent sign "All Adults Out" on the closed bedroom door a constant reminder that "Mother" can enter by invitation only!

A short time ago Justine slept on the streets of London. Admittedly it was a sponsored sleep-out for the homeless. Nevertheless, I had a restless Saturday night, made worse by the phone call from Andy, her youth worker. He and Justine were making their way to the local A&E department. She had fallen and had badly damaged two fingers. A quick chat with Justine soon ascertained that despite the accident she was in good spirits and had absolutely no intention of returning home. This was an emergency, but she still spurned the suggestion that I rush to her aid!

Seven o'clock on Sunday morning and the Mother was greeted by a smelly, tired, but happy teenager, who proudly announced that the right-hand finger was fractured, the left-hand finger broken, and that she and her mates had stayed awake all night! Not only had this been the best night of her life, but the reality of not being able to do any written work at school on Monday was an added bonus! All this said, she promptly collapsed in the car. After a short "conversation-free" drive home, the daughter headed straight for her bedroom (firmly shutting the door behind her!), never to surface for the rest of the day!

I'm told this is the behaviour of a normal, well-balanced teenager, and I'm happy to be the mother of this particular one ... and as Justine is still too young to hold a full driving license and partake in full-time work, I comfort myself with the fact that I am still of some use to her, even if it is as cash dispenser and driver.

Martine McCutcheon

MARTINE MCCUTCHEON was born to Jenny and John on 14 May 1976, and, with her sister Isla and little brother LJ, grew up in east London – good preparation, perhaps, for her future role as Tiffany in the BBC's *EastEnders*.

> When I was fourteen my father was so ignorant I could scarcely bear to have him around me. By the time I'd reached twenty-one I was amazed how much the old boy had learned.
>
> – *Mark Twain*

I can vividly remember how hard my Mum worked in order to give me the things I wanted as a child. Like most children, I believed that everything came so easy.

Mum worked very hard at three jobs. I wanted desperately to have a pair of disco roller-skates for Christmas, and I discovered that Mum had bought them early and hidden them under the bed.

As a child that could not wait, I sought them out and put them on. Mum was busy in the garden, and

I thought a quick whizz round the bedroom would do no harm.

I was discovered. Mum was furious. She had saved so hard to make my Christmas special, and I had ruined it. For the first time ever, Mum started to cry with sheer disappointment in me. I was thoroughly ashamed.

Long after this, when I got my first Saturday job, I decided to make amends and bought Mum a roller-skate key-ring. It was amazing. She immediately remembered the situation, hugged me and said, "You have grown up just how I wanted you to. Thoughtful, and remembering the lessons in life that I have tried to teach you."

I try never to take anything for granted now, and I certainly know that nothing ever comes that easy anymore.

John Harvey-Jones

SIR JOHN HARVEY-JONES was born in London on 16 April 1924 and served in the Royal Navy during the Second World War in submarines and naval intelligence. One of Britain's best-known industrialists, he has received many honorary degrees and awards for outstanding management, is involved in a number of charitable trusts, and is familiar to the general public for his *Troubleshooter* series on television. He married Mary in 1947 and they have one daughter.

Some parents have to go through times of incredible worry and distress. It is at times like these when it is so important for those around the parents, like employers and friends, to understand what is happening and to help out however they can. Sir John Harvey-Jones wrote to us to tell of a time that drew his family together in a way he could never have expected.

I suppose the strongest memory of my life regarding my family was when my daughter Gabrielle caught the polio virus – ironically within the first year of the introduction of the Salk vaccine. She was taken from us and put into an isolation hospital in Hither Green. At the time I was working at the

Admiralty on highly secret work. Life being what it is, at that particular moment I was involved in an operation for which I was personally responsible and the Admiralty was thoroughly unhelpful, refusing to give me any time off to be with my daughter or my wife. She was therefore left to cope with the whole strain and pressure on her own. When I was allowed out for a few hours we spent every moment we could at the isolation hospital – although very little visiting was allowed. It is difficult to describe the pressures on a family in these circumstances. From the onset of the disease there is absolutely nothing you can do – you have to watch its inexorable effects on your loved one, and you are all too aware that there is a strong likelihood of permanent paralysis or even of death. There is little or no chance of complete recovery from it. My wife, in my view, was nothing less than a heroine at that time. How she managed to keep the whole lot of us going and appearing to have belief and confidence in the future made me even more thankful that I had been lucky enough to meet and marry her. My daughter and her well-being became a total focus for all of us from then on and over a period of time I believe that this served to strengthen what was already a very strong and involved family group.

Spike Milligan

SPIKE MILLIGAN CBE comes from an army family and was born on 16 April 1918. Although he has written numerous popular books of humour and poetry, he is still best remembered by many people for his part in the *Goon Show*. He has a son and three daughters by his first wife, who died in 1978, and in 1983 he married his present wife Shelagh.

SEPTEMBER 3rd, 1939. The last minutes of peace ticking away. Father and I were watching Mother digging our air raid shelter. "She's a great little woman", said Father. "And getting smaller all the time", I added. Two minutes later, a man called Chamberlain, who did Prime Minister impressions, spoke on the wireless; he said, "As from eleven o'clock we are at war with Germany." (I loved the WE.) "War?" said Mother. "It must have been something we said", said Father. The people next door panicked, burnt their Post Office books and took in the washing.

Roy Castle

by ROB PARSONS

With a career that stretched to almost fifty years, ROY CASTLE was one of the UK's best-loved entertainers. Roy's *Record Breakers* TV shows, which he presented for twenty-two series, started in 1972 and gained Roy no fewer than eight listings in the *Guinness Book of Records*. These include the world's fastest tap dancer (twenty-four beats per second!) forty-three different instruments played in four minutes while continuing the same tune, and a three-hour twenty-three-minute wing-walk from London to Paris. In March 1992, Roy was diagnosed as having lung cancer. During his illness he was told about the lack of research into lung cancer, the huge number of people who contract the disease each year and the appalling survival rates. Strengthened by his strong Christian faith, Roy was determined to do everything possible to ensure that the cure for this disease is found as soon as possible. Consequently, joining forces with the Lung Cancer Fund, The Roy Castle Cause for Hope Appeal was formed. The appeal's aim was to raise £12 million to build the world's first international lung cancer research centre. His final public appearance was *The Littlewoods Tour of Hope*, which raised over £1.3 million towards lung cancer research. Just six weeks after ending the tour, Roy died at home. His wife Fiona told the waiting press, "No flowers, no mourning, no fuss, just lots of joy".

*F*AMILY was very important to Roy. Shortly before his death we were chatting at his home and he told me that when his children were young he always cleaned their shoes. He said, "You begin life with one pair of shoes by the bed, then two pairs, and then little shoes join the house, and then they get bigger and eventually leave until finally you're down to two pairs again, and then ... one pair."

I was staying the night with the Castles and when I couldn't sleep I began to write a poem about Roy and the shoe cleaning. The next morning over breakfast I read it to him. It must have touched him because some months later I went to watch him at the London Palladium and lo and behold he read the poem on stage!

For his Christmas present his daughter Antonia raided all the photograph albums in the loft and cut out some of the feet. She arranged the shoes around the poem and it hangs in their hall today.

My Family

I always cleaned the childrens' shoes,
The little (tiny!), patent shoes,
That covered feet fresh out of booties,
Cleaned the black and made it shine,
Removing final traces of stewed prune,
And other culinary delights – known only to the very
    young.

And as they grew I cleaned a larger shoe.
Shoes that were strong enough to walk in (almost!)
Certainly strong enough for a toddler to take five steps
    ... and fall.

And then those first school shoes:
Shoes that led such little feet
Into a world full of such tomorrows.

And later shoes, the toes of which
Lost all their battles with footballs, gravel, and old tin
    cans –
New shoes, that looked old within a week.

I cleaned them all.

Roy Castle

And as each night I did the task,
A million memories came flooding back
And I remembered a man long gone
Would clean our shoes.
Six children in all – my father cleaned each one -
As I now shine these for mine.

But children grow
And shoes are for feet that move -
That take the boy into a man.
And I remember well, the evening that I came
With cloth and brush
As I had done so many times –
Only to discover that of course the shoes had gone.

But they will come again – those shoes
Come again to me – oh not for cleaning now –
Other hands have long since done that task.
No, they will bring a man to me and a woman
Holding the hands of tiny ones –
With little feet.

And young eyes will look up and say
"Grandpa – mummy said ... that you will clean my
    shoes."

– *Rob Parsons*

Kevin Keegan

KEVIN KEEGAN was a professional footballer from 1966 to 1984. Born 14 February 1951, he played for England 1973–82 and captained the national team from 1976 to 1982. He became manager of Newcastle United in 1992 and since 1997 has been chief executive of Fulham. He and his wife Jean, whom he married in 1974, have two daughters.

In busy lives we all find it hard to make time for those who matter to us and, even when we do have time to spend together, things don't always go the way that we expect them to.

Fulham Football Club

Craven Cottage, Stevenage Road, London SW6 6HH
Telephone: 0171-736 6561. Facsimile: 0171-731 7047

My job involves being away from my family a great
deal, but I feel that the days that we do spend together
– the two girls, Jean and myself – are even more
precious.

My story is about a funny incident that happened a
few years ago. My eldest daughter, Laura, was then
fifteen and Sarah was twelve. It was a lovely spring
day and we all decided to go out for a horse ride. At
the time our house was surrounded by beautiful coun-
tryside. I have to say that Jean and the girls ride out
regularly, but with my hectic schedule I hadn't been
horse riding for some time. However, seeing it as a
time to spend together I said I would give it a go.
Despite the sunny weather, we had had some heavy
downpours of rain in previous weeks so in parts it was
pretty heavy going. We had a lovely time, laughing
and chatting for an hour or so and on the last stretch
we decided to canter home. The girls were on their
two ponies, Jean was on her old mare, Hideout, and I
was riding Laura's Hanoverian, Dynamo. Hideout used
to get a little skittish at times, particularly if another
horse came up close behind her and Jean made me
aware of this fact as we broke into a canter. However,
Dynamo had other things on his mind – all he wanted

to do was catch Hideout and totally ignored any direction I tried to steer him in. As Hideout heard Dynamo thundering up behind her she immediately went into her version of a "bucking bronco" with poor Jean taken completely unawares, flying through the air and landing face first in the mud. Hideout at this stage saw home in sight and careered off down the park towards the stables. Dynamo, who must have thought he was missing out on the fun charged into top gear with me clinging on for dear life until I realised it would be much safer to bale out on to the soft mud, which I did.

By this time the girls were in hysterics (not laughing I might add), worrying about the horses disappearing at the far end of the field. Jean and I were covered in mud, looking very despondent, limping back to the stables and the girls' only concern was the horses! By the time we returned they were outside their stables with a smug look on their faces. Needless to say I haven't been riding since. I think I will stick to the four wheels rather than four legs and leave the horses to the girls. Of course we have laughed about it since but at the time, I assure you it was not funny!

The joys of family life!

Kevin Keegan
Chief Operating Officer

John Cole

JOHN COLE, born to George and Alice on 23 November 1927, has been a journalist all his life. From 1956 to 1975 he worked for the *Guardian* before becoming Deputy Editor of the *Observer* in 1976. From there he moved to the BBC in 1982 as Political Editor, a post he held until 1992. He married Margaret in 1956 and they have four sons.

Many of us would be satisfied just to get our children through the teenage years and into a life of their own. So when they go on to marry and have children, and a big family group gets together, it can be a recipe for some very special memories indeed ...

*F*OR our fortieth wedding anniversary in 1996, my wife conceived the idea of taking our whole family to the same hotel in the same resort, Dinard in Brittany, where she and I had spent part of our honeymoon. So we went, in four cars: Madge and myself, our four sons, three daughters-in-law, and (then) five grandchildren.

My wife, who is wiser than me, said we must not expect everybody to remain together for the week we were there; each family must do their own thing during the day, and we would come together at dinner-time.

In the event, everybody seemed to reach the same stretch of beach, about two minutes' walk from the hotel, around lunchtime, and a great feeding of the multitude on each other's bread, pâté, cheese and wine took place. On the actual anniversary, our daughters-in-law arranged cake and champagne on the beach.

Considering the grandchildren were aged from five years to five months, a considerable amount of communal swimming, football, long-jumping, and sand architecture took place. And the hotel staff, with the usual adaptability of the French, seemed to take it as normal that one family member should be absent having a nappy-change or other running repair at any given moment in the meal.

Encore des pommes frites, peut-être?

Rob Parsons

ROB PARSONS was a senior partner of a large provincial legal
practice. He left this position in 1988 to form the charity Care
for the Family, of which he is now an Executive Director. He
is the best-selling author of *The Sixty Minute Father* and *The
Sixty Minute Marriage*.

W HEN my son Lloyd was fifteen we were on
holiday together and came across some
people fishing on a lake. He was keen to try his hand
but not only did we have no rod but I had never
been fishing in my life. Lloyd was determined to try
it and found a long stick and a piece of string. We
put a safety pin on the end, to which we attached a
large lump of bread. If you are opposed to angling
let me reassure you that never in the history of the
world have fish been so safe; they discussed the
bread, they broke bits off, they shared it out among
their friends.

I noticed other "proper" anglers sneering at us
and it annoyed me. I told Lloyd to wait by the lake
while I stalked across a road to a restaurant, outside
of which, I had earlier noticed, there were whole fish
laid out. I bought one; it cost me almost £3.00.

I rammed in on the hook, threw it in the water, and said to Lloyd, "When some people come past I want you to yell, 'Dad, I think you've got one!'" He gave me a sympathetic look, and said, "Okay."

Minutes later I heard him whisper, "Get ready, Dad, here come some people." I tensed myself and gave him the nod. "Dad," he screamed at the top of his voice, "I think you've got one!"

The little crowd coming along the path heard Lloyd shout and turned to us; I yanked the line out of the water and turned to gloat. But they looked embarrassed and, heads down, they sidled off. I turned to ask my son what had gone wrong with our plan, but he was helpless with laughter; this boy was rolling in the grass. It took him several minutes before he could speak but eventually he spluttered it out. "Two things were wrong, Dad. First: it looked dead – you should have jiggled the line a bit, but best of all – you had put the hook through its *tail*."

My second story is one of the reasons I wrote The Sixty
Minute Father *– urging fathers not to miss their kids'
childhood.*

*M*Y daughter, Kate, is now twenty-one years old,
but I remember her so clearly as a small child.
Some nights I'd be reading her a bedtime story when
suddenly I'd hear the phone ringing downstairs.
She'd say, "Please leave it, Dad." She may as well
have asked me to fly. "I'll only be a moment!" I'd
shout, as I took the stairs three at a time.

That one call would often lead to another and
then suddenly I'd remember I'd not got the frog back
into a prince and I'd rush back upstairs, but little
eyes had fought to stay awake as long as they could.

The tragedy of that story is that I've been a senior
partner in a busy legal practice, I'm an author, I run
seminars all around the world and in those contexts
I have had thousands of business calls, many of
which have been described as "urgent". I honestly
can't remember *one* that couldn't have waited five
minutes.

Jonathan Edwards

JONATHAN EDWARDS was born on 10 May 1966 and is Britain's top triple-jumper. He won the World Championships in 1995 and took a Silver Medal at the 1996 Olympics. He and his wife Alison have two sons.

Perhaps it is fitting to end with this contribution, which sums up our theme – that great memories, even those of extraordinary people, are built upon lots and lots of very ordinary moments ...

I think, for us, that the most special things about family life are the familiar routines. These rather than the "one off" occasions, are what make families what they are (or aren't). My relationship with Alison, and our relationships with our boys, Samuel and Nathan, are built around the humdrum of everyday life rather than unique events. Of course, my initial thought when Fiona asked me to write a few words about our family was to try and remember some particular significant/funny incident that would really grab the attention of the readers and yet the more I reflected, I realised that the Edwards family is what it is because of the bath-time routine and the inevitable "discussion" of who mummy is going to dry and who gets the "short straw" and daddy doing the honours. Or because of the bed-time ritual, and Nathan wanting the same story he has had for the last three months (note: special does not always mean enjoyable!). And the dreaded morning-time when, after several attacks to get into mum and dad's bed have been repelled, they eventually make it in – cold feet and all! And I could go on and on, but I think you get the picture. We do have many special "one offs" to remember, but the love commitment we have toward one another, the things that make us a family, have been born out of sharing the "everyday" together.

Sources

Gloria Hunniford (from *Gloria*, autobiography)

Nelson Mandela (from his autobiography, *Long Walk to Freedom*)

Bill Cosby (from *Childhood*, Bantam Press, 1991)

Sir David Frost (from *An Autobiography – From Congregations to Audiences*, HarperCollins, 1993)

Dickie Bird ('Twelve Songs IX' from *Collected Poems* by W. H. Auden, Faber and Faber, used with permission)

Frank Bruno (from *Eye of the Tiger*, Weidenfeld and Nicolson, London)

Lynda Lee-Potter (by courtesy of the *Daily Mail*)

Spike Milligan (from *Adolf Hitler – My Part in his Downfall*, Michael Joseph, London)

All other contributions appear for the first time in this book and are reproduced from original letters sent to Fiona Castle and Rob Parsons.

A Note about Care for the Family

The charity CARE FOR THE FAMILY was established in 1988. Its headquarters are in Cardiff and there is a staff of fifty, plus volunteers. Its aim is to strengthen families by providing education, training and ongoing support. While this often involves working with families who are experiencing very difficult situations, at least half of its resources are spent on "prevention".

In the past decade, over two hundred thousand people have attended seminars on marriage, parenting, and other family issues. Thousands of people write each year to request resources or seek help in dealing with concerns ranging from marital problems to bullying at school.

Care for the Family's activities and projects include:

- *Parents Who Care* – residential weekends for those facing particularly difficult parenting situations. Recent events have covered the issues of eating disorders, drugs, behavioural problems and dealing with the death of a child.
- *Take a Break!* – subsidised holidays designed for single parents.
- *Adventures in Parenting* – exciting holidays designed

to strengthen the relationship between children and parents. Following a Fathers and Sons weekend one father wrote in an article in the *Independent* newspaper:

> *I really enjoyed the experience of having time alone with Sam ... The activities and the challenge did bring us together.*

- *Parenting courses* – the *Parentalk* pack, filmed at GMTV studios, including individual course material and a leaders' guide for use in schools, parents and toddlers and other community groups.
- *Seminars* – over forty nationwide presentations a year, each attended by between 200 and 1,500 people.